I0623438

SLEEPING WITH GHOSTS

Sleeping with Ghosts

{ POEMS & MUSINGS BY JENNIFER A. PAYNE }

Branford, Connecticut 2024

© 2024, Jennifer A. Payne

All rights reserved. Please respect the copyright of this book — its contents reflect hours of creative effort, predawn conversations with muses, and hundreds of pots of coffee. We ask that you do not reproduce or translate this in any form or by any means, digital, electronic, or mechanical, including photocopying, recording, or by any information storage and retrieval system, without permission in writing or by email from the publisher, except for the use of brief quotations in a book review or related article. Thank you!

Cover art, Shadows, by Malgorzata Maj (Mrągowo, Poland)
Cover starshine graphic by Lana Elanor (Tulume, Mexico)
Same Time Next Year, Lilacs, from Shutterstock
All other chapter drawings by Michael Rayback (Kyiv, Ukraine)
Back cover photo, Full Moon, by Jen Payne

Book design by Words by Jen (Branford, CT)
Printed in the U.S.A. (I)

ISBN: 979-8-9901523-1-1

POETRY / MEMOIR

Three Chairs

Three Chairs Publishing
P.O. Box 453
Branford, CT 06405

www.3chairspublishing.com

"Don't tell me how to grieve. Don't tell me ghosts fade away eventually, like they do in movies, waving goodbye with see-through hands. Lots of things fade away but ghosts like these don't, heartbreak like this doesn't."

— Anthony Doerr, *Memory Wall*

"Soulmates aren't the ones who make you happiest, no. They're instead the ones who make you feel the most. Burning edges and scars and stars. Old pangs, captivation, and beauty. Strain and shadows and worry and yearning. Sweetness and madness and dreamlike surrender. They hurl you into the abyss. They taste like hope."

— Victoria Erickson, *Edge of Wonder: Notes from the Wildness of Being*

Readers say Jen Payne is "a master at storytelling who brings us to the realization that the stories she shares are actually ours." Her poems are "funny, sad, sexy, maddening"

"*Sleeping with Ghosts*, the deeply personal new collection of Jen Payne's work, is introduced with a poem about Kintsugi, the Japanese art of repairing broken pottery in which the seams are decorated with lacquer mixed with gold or silver dust. In the poem, as in the entire collection, we are invited to examine, to touch, and to feel the gold-etched evidence of the poet's own richly lived experience. Beautifully crafted and luminous, these poems take the reader on an intimate and unforgettable journey of love found and lost, the joys of creativity, and the power of memory."

> — Judith K. Liebmann, Ph.D., Poet Laureate of Branford, Connecticut, author of the poetry collection *Ekphrasis*

"Payne's latest collection of poems, musings, and artwork is a bouquet of balloons — lovers, friends, and moments she could let slip away but that she keeps close through her writing about them....the poems let readers into a delicate and secret balance between worlds. Like one poem about a dream lingering into wake-time, the collection is liminal, linking opposites: definite and indefinite, reality and fantasy, timeless and time-specific, and indescribable and descriptive."

> — Mari Carlson, *US Review of Books*

"*Sleeping with Ghosts* is not an ordinary ghost tale. Jen Payne's combination of transparency and opaqueness teases the reader with sometimes wistful, other times gnawing, reflections on encounters with lovers and soulmates. Beautifully written with her captivating twist and cadence of words and endings, Jen's latest collection of writings is a poignant meditation on a life of love confronted."

> — Mary O'Connor, author of *Say Yes! to Your Creative Self* and *Passing Shadows*

"As you might infer from the title, this poet is gifted with a sense of irony, catalogues the ghosts of relationships lost which visit her still with hard-earned honesty bereft of self-pity, wonderful imagery and, somehow, a lightness of touch. She describes with deft strokes more than her share of visiting ghosts. But she allows them their charms where deserved, and we are happy to travel the long- and near-past with her as she sheds one interesting character after another. We find ourselves not just admiring but also delighting in her as she moves through good times and hard with a poet's kind of vision and language and a perspective equal parts wise and whimsical."

— Nancy Fitz-Hugh Meneely, author,
  Simple Absence and *Letter from Italy, 1944*

"What I love most about *Sleeping with Ghosts* is how it leaves room for each of us to find our own story within its pages. These poems don't just tell Jen's story — they remind us to revisit our own past, to honor our own scars, and maybe to find a bit of poetry there, too.... If you're ready to take a thoughtful, heartfelt stroll through memory and meaning, *Sleeping with Ghosts* is absolutely worth your time. Jen's gentle but honest voice will stay with you long after the last page is turned."

— Kaecey McCormick, writer, Former Poet Laureate Cupertino,
  CA, 2023 Connecticut Poetry Award Winner

"In its reflective tone and exploration of love, loss, and memory, this book is the perfect companion for nights when the mid mind wanders and the heart yearns for connection. Known for her work meditating on the external world, Jennifer Payne invites readers to look inward. In the wise and reflective collection, *Sleeping with Ghosts*, Payne creates and presents poems that reveal and introduce "ghosts," bringing the reader "into the heart and mind of a poet.""

— Alicia Gomez, The Book Nook, *Winter on the
  Shoreline Magazine*, Shore Publishing

To my lovers and soulmates,
muses and ghosts...

table of contents

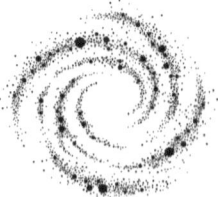

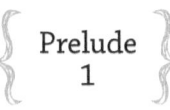

{ *Prelude* }

prelude

Kintsugi

come, look closely
I am gold here
in between the pieces

broken

no longer broken

repaired

each fine crack
part of my story

my shimmering self
my here-and-now

but there is no disguise

no pretending
you don't see the scar

it is the thick hot line
that shows you
how I traveled here

come, touch it
trace your finger
along its golden trail

there is poetry there,
can you feel it?

We Walk with Ghosts

On the trail we often walk,

we lovers and poets

of life and light,

I saw them once,

she with a summer hat

in shade and shadow,

he by her side, already eternal.

When she passed me

on the bridge,

I was casting stones,

but she was as solitary

as me by then,

missing love as much

and equally unrepentant.

prelude

Story Keeper: A 100-Word Story

I save their stories like scraps of stolen treasure. I know, for example, that she was conceived at the 1965 World's Fair, and that hidden above his left ear is a question-mark shaped scar. I remember the name of the child they lost, what she called the family dog, and that he wakes from nightmares as if in a back-alley brawl. Thief, collector, story keeper. How easily I recall their memories *and* mine — those couples in love and couples lost, the pillow talk of lovers, the half-life of trauma, and the white-haired widow forever chasing her dog by the shore.

The Poet at Midnight

Barefoot and moon-lit
she sneaks to the shed
to consider the
bucket of bones
she keeps on a shelf

picks at the
small white moments
she never thinks to bury

only to hold them again

turn them over
in her hand

press her thumb
into their curves
and brittle endings

remember sometimes
the soft flesh
that held them together once,
their silken wings of flight

oh how they soared!

When she is quiet enough
she hears them sing

whisper secrets
and stories
she saves in her pocket

shimmering

burning to be told

8

Star-crossed
ghost one

star-crossed

Star-Crossed: A 100-Word Story

I suppose I was a force to be reckoned with, even then at 19, when we stood in his driveway and I explained how my world was just bigger than his, and I drew wide circles in the air like the orbits of planets. But he loved me then, loved how we could talk for hours with only the stars as witness, loved that I loved him back in those brief, sweet moments we traveled around each other. In the end, he was the first one with courage enough to propose something more...and I wonder *what if*...sometimes...like a comet, fleeting.

Act One. Final Scene.
August 1986

It's dark, summertime-late, right before the semester starts. She's driven 40 miles on backroads in the pouring rain to see him. It's been almost a year. He's working, but she had no choice. She has to do this, even if it's hard to breathe.

He can't believe she's standing in the doorway. It's been almost a year. Is that rain or tears? He tells her he can take his break, meet her outside, but as soon as she leaves, he panics. Can't breathe. Worries she'll drive away. So he grabs a plastic-wrapped bouquet by the cash register and runs out — leaves customers waiting in line.

Cars on the wet, weathered pavement. Lights like stars. The windows fog up, blurry — like a dream — as she watches him run towards her, startles when the door opens fast and he jumps in. Rain or tears? He hands her daisies. He loves me. He loves me not. "Tomorrow?" she asks.

star-crossed

"Tomorrow," he says. Five minutes. Ten. There's nothing else to say. They both know he gets married in the morning. This is just goodbye. Again.

They sit facing each other, silent for a while. The windshield wipers count time like her heartbeats. Five minutes. Ten. He starts to leave, then pulls her close, winds his fingers through her hair and kisses her, hard and forever.

"Forever," he says, before he runs back out into the rain.

She had no choice.

On the Death of a Friend, 1988

Of course you were the one to call.
It was late, I remember,
a rainy night like the last time we met.
Cars on the wet, weathered pavement,
wipers marking time.
Starshine in puddles and you,
light years away,
saying you knew I'd want to know,
knew he'd been important.
You knew, despite the distance in our orbits,
despite the final, fervent kiss
that birthed a galaxy between us.

My heart.

You knew.

Time Traveler, 2013

He arrives across a wasteland of time
in accelerated motion   lights   moving swiftly
like Roddenberry's hallucinations.

Resistance is futile in the face of such memory,
as this time traveler pulls strings of moments from gray
    matter

string theory:
           we are all connected

As he is to me, I am to him and to you and to all
by threads of stories we tell each other here, now
in this space   time   continuum

    Addendum

How we shapeshift —
reconsider, reevaluate —
move warp-speed from present to past to future.

That superposition feeds poetry and soul —
but my heart is here sweet time traveler   *here*

What comes next?

And He Will Shout It from the Rafters

it required no acrobatic maneuver
no perfectly perfected prose,
or metered response

there was no need to hold back,
contrive, force, restrain, bide —
no contortionists need apply

she did not walk the tightrope
the gangplank, on eggshells —
the way was clear and easy

and he offered no illusion,
sleight of hand, trickery —
what you see is what you get

step right up, don't be shy
don't be jaded, cynical,
doubtful

skeptic!

he loves her,
he just loves her,
and he will shout it from the rafters

16

There Is No Synonym for Reunion

I wanted my skin to be soft,
so you couldn't feel the years between us.
I thought that might preclude
the inevitable side effects of time travel.
That if Now were soft and loving,
maybe Then wouldn't matter.

But it wasn't Then I needed to worry about.

The prime directive of time travel says:
time changes everything and nothing
No matter how soft my skin,
how sweet the intention,
the truth of what Is
eviscerates everything.

We have been here before.

Litmus Test

He said he drove a thousand miles
the night he thought my car crashed,
came despite the false alarm
despite the decade passed,
said he'd do it again
if I was in trouble
if I'd only ask

Of course, it was all illusion
that beautiful shapeshifting dance,
a conjuring of dreams
and rose-colored romance,
a shimmering potion
of might-have-beens
of what-if and circumstance

But he said he'd drive a thousand miles
and even now, it makes me smile.

star-crossed

Stargazer

The man who
loved me forever
told me once
he slept on
Cherokee ground,
under a tent
made of stars,
     dreaming of me

It was mythology
of course —
his and mine.
An optical illusion,
those celestial bodies
forever rising
to dance
across the sky

We were the ones moving
slowly slowly slowly apart,
from that first, brief collision
now ever only starstuff

    dusting
       memories
          and poems

Seeing Red
ghost two

New Hampshire, 1992

Do you remember the day we saw the lupines?
That hidden meadow behind the undulating
    ribbon of pine?
We saw it at the same time, and you pulled
    over before I had to ask.
Lupines as far as our eyes could see!
It felt magical and romantic and just for us.

Everything that weekend was just for us —
the snow on summer mountains,
that perfect campfire,
the moose sighting and chipmunk troupe,
the strawberry moon and breathtaking stars.

It was everything I loved most about us —
our heart place, you and me on the open road,
cold air and coffees, Tull on the radio,
the banks and curves of conversation.

I never think about the other things —
the things that melt snow and douse dreams,
the things that scorch fields of flowers from memory.

Raspberries

This was the Sunday drive
on an s-shaped back road
slithering to a horizon
that loomed ahead of us:
you, me, your kids in the backseat
    frightened.

When you finally stopped
it was to steal fruit
from a sharp shrub,
our hearts pounding,
feet bound, fingers stained

Red, the taste of summer berries
and buried fear
simmering in a pot for jam.

Breath Counting

When sleeping with a bear
it is critical to pay attention to the breath —
his and yours.

His will tell you when it is safe
to muck about in dreams
and when it is time
to curl up and play dead.

Death
     in this case: to feign sleep
is a practiced thing

slow   deep   breath   in
slow   deep   breath   out
slow   deep   breath   in
slow   deep   breath   out

Most nights, he'll forget his hunger
and roll over — you pray
hands folded around your knees
making yourself small
a burr in the blanket and of far less importance
than himself and his sleep.

seeing red

New Haven Harbor, 1994

This is the moment of leaving,
this view out the passenger window,
a sideways glance, passing
rain as falling stars on glass
belie any reminder of wishes,
this is just the falling part —
the out of, away from, apart part,
watching with envy
how the tugs push
the things that cannot move,
how once unburdened
this becomes that,
how easily the plane departs,
lights, too, like stars,
moving toward the horizon.

Rockport

It was Rockport, North Shore
right before the fall
that humid, hot July,

the slow seduction
of an afternoon,
swimming and showers
that enticed hours
of love making,

our voracious race
for sustenance —
four courses and wine,
Garth and *The Dance*
played on the deck
there on Bearskin Neck.

We were finished, even then
and we knew it,
held tight and played pretend
that one last weekend,
love and loss and relief writhing
beneath summer cotton,
our consummated Goodbyes.

seeing red

Same Time Next Year
ghost three

Liaison

She pressed against him
in the shadowed corner,
kissed his shy, curious lips
asked but didn't beg
and made him blush
redder than a fine glass of wine

but it was more potent than fine,
deep and sensual,
with notes of collusion
that sparked on their tongues

interest begat affirmation
assignations
assumed
(hoped for)
and then
beneath the loyal stars
a secret handshake
shhhhhh!
and plans to meet again
same time, next year

at which they both arrived
dressed to the nines
alter egos
bewitched by chemistry
and dance beats
(or heartbeats)
long into the sleepless night

same time next year

liaisons ensued for years
often long distance
consummated as
paper promises
burned after reading

or rendezvous
with hard to conceal
anticipation
clandestine
and yet
undisguised
and fully transparent

the affair stamped
TOP SECRET
from that very first kiss
in the shadows,
but not for them
when everything was shared
naked, not in whispers

Light Years from Lilac Sunday

this is it, Memory,
that day when lilacs bloom
and I think of him   of us
our trespass in the arbor
boughs so heavy with starlight
we felt drunk
when those first unexpected kisses
found places in the sky and he named them
like he named the flowers and trees
his fingers marked the heavens
the branch, the blossom,
the small of my back so
still, now, a trace remains
forever notes
the day when lilacs bloom
and we made you, Memory,
light years from now,
never love   never nothing
just a sweet, sweet something in between.

same time next year

I Prayed He Left More than a Spoon
(or The Last Time We Met)

As the sun rose, he whispered,
I'll come back if I've left anything
then packed and went
as quickly as he did that first time
some ten years before.
It was graduation then —
this time a funeral.
No lingering, not like the years in between
when we dozed dream-wrapped
late into the morning   loved.
But with such a long ride away
from our reverie,
he left before we had a chance to...

    a chance to say anything more than

Same time next year?
Should I bake a cake?
I'll come back if I've left anything.

I prayed he left more than a spoon,
held my breath in pregnant pause for weeks
until it was clear there was nothing
to come back to   not even the spoon
which still makes its way into coffee,
stirs up that morning
and what might have been   after all
had he left anything more.

Love Story Lost

These are the days

I remember him most.

Lilacs bloom

at the corner,

and all the world

is full of promise.

This Fine Green Ribbon
for delinda

Cape Cod Sunrise, Almost

The sun's gone missing, darling,
and you, two thousand miles away,
    are missing too
        from this solitary east coast shore,
    and yet there we are
    in more than memory
walking that Gulf Coast beach
pitch dark, single file, you in the lead
    fearless, I think,
    as always
    pulling me along
as we giggle stumble across the shell-full sand
that one angel feather
    that stabs itself between my toes
before we find a place
to lay down our blanket,
    sip hot coffee,
knee against knee and
arm against arm
like sisters
quiet and waiting
waiting for the start of a day
    that never comes, save for
gray against gray and
pearl against pearl
until we make our way back
holding hands and laughing at the folly.

Blue Moon (or Time Finds
Us Again in Honfleur)

The wide, whorled moon shell
n'est pas bleu
it's chalk-white and shattered
so only the round face gazes
at me from the rough-washed sand
here, four thousand days away —
on this full moon, blue moon way.
Here, where, in our future perfect
we will have sat by the quay, again,
eaten mussels in that broth with wine
sun on our travel-weary faces,
facing Le Vieux-Bassin
your smiling moon face
what I will have remembered most,
a rare find among the ebb and flow
of this dream-whorled world.

Heist

I drove the get-away car that day,
left it on idle in the parking space
closest to the electronic OUT door
of Porter's Grocery there in Alpine.

It was a bright Texas day, hot
the car angled in shade just enough
for a clear-on view of the lobby,
bulletin board, the poster, tacks, and tape.

We'd scoped out the joint before,
cased the aisles for jerky
and bottles of wine for dinner
back in Marfa at the Thunderbird.

There was a nice patio
outside our room with blue lights,
like the alien spaceships
you could see there sometimes?

Funny things in that part of Texas:
spaceships and meteors,
a roadside Prada shoe outlet,
Chinati's take on art, and ours.
Ours was *Viva Terlingua!*
her bright red cowboy hat
hand-strung turquoise beads and
that witty West Texas smile.

It's a smile that says just about all
you want to say about West Texas,
about the wild Trans-Pecos
and its wide expanse of stars.

It's a promise of whiskey at La Kiva,
or hot coffee while the sun rises
over Terlingua and Study Butte
over Big Bend and the Rio Grande.

It's a smile that remembers solitude,
the promise of oddity and isolation,
of community, maybe, companionship —
two friends on the road laughing.

It's the awesome sound a car makes solo
on a nighttime desert highway,
or peeling out from Porter's,
Viva Terlingua! rolled up in the back seat.

37

Ode to My Ghost at Terlingua
(or You Just Keep on Pushing
My Love Over the Borderline)

Is it OK to set good boundaries
even as we forgive those who trespass against us

How does one love with an open heart
without one's heart on her sleeve
or worse yet
leave it precariously propped
against a stone gathering moss
unmoving
and
unyielding

How do we
cut ties with all the lies
understand that blood is thicker than water
but to relieve pressure, one must cut deep
a necessary wound
the beginning cause of these endings

And if thy right hand offend thee,
cut it off, and cast it from thee

Cut and cut and cut
Until there is nothing and no one
except pieces of forgotten poetry taped
to the adobe brick wall of the home
I make on the shore of her desert
wide and without fences

cigarettes and whiskey and only

and only

the sound of stars.

40

Water Under the Bridge
ghost four

Under His Spell
(or I am Sure He Was a Sorcerer)

I saw him fly once
up a steep flight of stairs.
I tried to outrun him
(but wasn't too scared).

Watched him drive blind
down a street's wrong side —
from a kiss no less.
(I was there for the ride.)

He vanished like ghosts,
gone for weeks, not days.
Drove into a tree once,
walked away unscathed.

He's cheated death and watched death
and wrestled it in the street,
he's had past lives and nine lives,
and one I'll never meet.

His devil's smile and demon laugh
they melted me every time.
Telepath, empath —
I swear he read my mind.

water under the bridge

He foretold our future
in such hypnotic prose,
then all of it came true.
(or mostly, I suppose).

He was impulse, reactive
conniving, and wild,
charming, seductive,
I was broken, beguiled —

So I ate all his lies
(and fed all his fears).
My heart craved the magic,
But his love cost me years.

water under the bridge

Codepend-dance

I told him once it was a dance,
and I hyphenated
the push – pull – come – go
choreography
like any limber poet might.
How clever the analogy!

(And how could he not love clever?)

Watch me pirouette, I said.
Put a spin on this
so the song doesn't end,
and the routine goes on forever.

(Did you see that? Clever again.)

It's the same old song and dance, love.
We can't side-step the family dance-step,
it's in our genes, and I don't mean Kelly, so...

I'd like to shake things up a bit,
you know, move with the times...
Why not dance this year's dance to —
the Pachanga.

Just Once in a Very Blue Moon

I found your letter in my mailbox today
You were just checkin' if I was okay
And if I miss you
Well you know what they say…

The playlist doesn't know better
Picks a song from the queue —
picks *you* from the queue —
and it's a blue-moon moment
just yesterday:

4 a.m. on the Expressway
up and around the city,
before they buried all of
the late night stories
beneath monuments of hours

The car is cold,
a late winter bite in the air
and pale smoke curls —
that habit more forgot than you now —

water under the bridge

a pinpoint moment
I hear an angel's voice,
clear and bright, sing
of longing and memory
those moments of missing
that arrive at random,
sometimes, like now
a hundred years since then...

you, me, our mess of love
piercing the darkness then,
this rainy afternoon now
and I am celestial,
my heart traveling time

Just once in a very blue moon
And I feel one comin' on soon

Water Under the Bridge: 15 Years Fast Forward

She was sitting at the bar, 7:30.

She turned to watch for him and their eyes met.

His look said There you are! How could I not recognize you? and his smile...
>   *that smile*

She imagined the people sitting nearby watched them in awe.

She imagined the moment surrounded them with white light.
>   *she imagined so much*

Their eyes never lost touch.

They sat and talked and laughed for hours.

He reached for her hand as if he had done so every day since they last saw each other.

water under the bridge

That affinity surprised them long into the night.

There was lightning in the winter sky.

They kissed
        and he tasted like hope...

But slowly, something old and murky seeped in.

It reeked of sadness and hurt and guilt and fear.

It was all of the things they hadn't said,
and all of the stories they hadn't remembered.

It breached a gap so wide there was
no way for her to reach him.

She could feel him leaving.
        again

She could feel it before either
of them knew he would.

There Were Other Words for This, Not Love

I rarely thought of that night in the gatehouse that
overlooked the Sound, salt air moist on lips, and wine.

You wore a white sweater, the kind mariners wear
while they tear hooks from small fish and throw them
overboard.

There was a fire in the fireplace, and you sat on the floor
next to me with your arm around my shoulders, laughing.

I can still see your face, that smirk of a smile that made
my heart swim; feel the spot in my chest where love and
anxiety mixed often with you.

There was a white robe in your bathroom, a second
toothbrush in a cup — the things a woman leaves behind
when she is certain she will not be discarded.

They were not mine.

My things were in a pile on the floor next to your bed
where you left me in the dark, gutted and alone — the
sound of a door somewhere shutting.

water under the bridge

What if LA LA LA Is My Superpower?

When he said he never understood
how I could LA LA LA about things
I thought, now that's ironic
because I was never very LA LA LA about him
I was more OH MY GOD and OH NO! and WHAT NOW?
But OH NO! always has a way of morphing into
     OH WELL when the adrenaline wears off
and there's no choice but to change pace,
switch things up
MAKE LEMONADE NOT WAR
paint the dining room blue
sing *Give Me Novocaine* until the pain wears off
then get right back on the proverbial horse
and ride off into the sunset,
hope and optimism in a pocket
red cape fluttering in the wind
singing

LA LA LA

Afterword

Her first husband was a rogue
too young for what she had in mind
but it was high-school sweetheart love
and her parents insisted
in a Roman Catholic sort of way
his too, it was a good investment
that soon included the benchmark 2.0 kids
in a house-and-white-picket-fence world
but he was prone to outrageous fortunes
and accidental accidents
that left him nearly speechless
her too, most nights, waiting by the phone
so she gave herself a Divorce for Christmas
and never, ever looked back.

He did. Retraced his missteps
relived his worst nightmares (and mine)
hit rewind and started over
with a nimble bride the same age
his first wife had been
though a better investment this time
consented not contrived
with two more dividends and
a house on a Dream
where he sometimes smiles
that scoundrel smile
to his reflection in the mirror
a flash of wicked conceit
for an endgame so very well played.

Wednesdays
ghost five

wednesdays

On the First Day

"Be sure of your intentions,"
she says to his advances.

Because I am about to devour you.

She doesn't tell him that.
She doesn't need to.

They are about to devour each other —
consume, engulf, ravage, ruin,

love

You see, she wants someone to love her forever,
and he needs someone to love him right now;

She wants to believe there will be no end,
and he needs there to be no consequence;

so she is the one who asserts the first kiss,
and he is the one who never looks back.

The Fall

Are you sure?

she asks in a whisper.

Nodding, he sets

his hand against

the small of her back,

pulling her towards him

until they disappear —

falling stars

headfirst.

First Revelation

His touch —
softly down to
secret places —
was not as hungry
as I expected.

There was no rush
to grab hold
of the moment,
to take
for himself
its brass ring.

In the last light of day
he was unhurried
and gentle,
savoring the slow,
easy pace of us.

So many
sweet unspokens
found audience
across skin that night,
they surprised
a rapt applause.

Waiting,

she

pulled

the

pearls

around

her

neck

counting

moments

on

them

like

a

rosary

penance

for

filling

her

emptiness

with

him.

wednesdays

Just Forget the World: A 100-Word Story

They were travelers on a late rainy night, two old
souls stopped for a cup of coffee at some all-night
waystation. Strangers but familiar, they seemed
destined to be there together. So they leaned in for
comfort, watched the storm from the refuge of a
booth they shared for a while. The jukebox played
Chasing Cars, and they — enveloped by a blanket
of conversation and laughter — drank from a deep,
intimate brew of secrets. They embraced, held each
other one last time; whispered "thank you for coming
into my life," as the rain let up enough for them to
leave.

At the Confluence of Beliefs

I call it magic, so easily seduced am I by lost slippers and kisses that wake the dead.

You, hocus pocus and nothing more, though the charm you wear tells me you believe in something. *Something.*

Surely you do, because faith holds you fast in firmament I will never know.

Once upon a dream I thought I did...

Perhaps I should resign myself to bone and afterlife,

a reliquary for your soul to recognize

so we can conjure something more...

next time.

wednesdays

In Love with Ghosts

Surely it is no secret —
I am in love with ghosts.
Just this morning I awoke with one
curled naked against my spine
on the sheets I bought just for you.
In those short-film dreams before dawn,
we were there again
both holy and transparent —
as ghosts are known to be.
But life is never that see-through, is it?
Rarely that ethereal.
For here we are bound —
so bound —
to the day-to-day,
dreams tucked away in linen closets,
square corners and pedestrian piles.

Resolve

When he left, I anointed myself in sandalwood,

dabbed oil on pulse points still timed to his heart.

If he could no longer hold me, I would let go —

assume the forest as his embrace,

place feet firmly once more on this small satellite
ever spinning, ever changing.

Wednesday

It was just the other summer day
I wondered if your hair turned gray.

If you loved her still enough to stay.

And then as if on cue today,
I saw your car go by my way.
That telltale glance gave you away,
the smile that always could betray.

And I, with so much left to say
kept still and let this poem aweigh.

The Road to Damascus

At the intersection
of what was wrong
I am so sorry.
and what was right
I have no regrets.

there is the crossing
of love and loss,
of sorrow and deep affection —

a stand-still moment:

the call to pause

the world moves past

the clock ticks

and in the gesture
of a wave
we touch time
and make amends

wednesdays

I Dream about Us Dancing

When we first met,
I dreamt about your hands.
There were so many reasons not to,
    but I did.

There was never anything illicit.
Simple gestures of affection:
a handshake or hand on my arm,
a touch of my shoulder.

It's been years since then,
but I still dream about your hands.
There are so many reasons not to,
    but I do.

There's never anything illicit.
Simple gestures between strangers:
some event years from now,
your hand on my back as the music plays.

I am a rock. I am an island.

ghost six

68   i am a rock i am an island.

In the Wake of Fantasía
(South Florida)

his lips would taste of lime
and crushed mint   warm like añejo rum

his kisses like poetry
Neruda nuzzled between breasts
Cortázar caressing pale thighs

afternoons in the shade of
palm trees, shutters barely
masking heat   and storm

full to the margin and
neverending like Márquez
words spilled on silk

the air sweet and
heavy like tobacco
in the aftermath: red wine

Hemingway out loud
ripe fruits on a platter, dripping

Online and Unrequited

Borrowed poetry

rings false to ears I adore

and dangles in the ethernet,

flaccid — like my dignity.

I caught him on a pragmatic day

when he is nothing but my antithesis,

so we hunt-and-peck

to dissect my intentions.

Tomorrow he might find he loves me again

and add more exes and ohs to his reply.

But for now, I give up and type

what I meant to say was

have a nice day.

i am a rock i am an island.

grab *v.* to take or seize by or as if by a sudden motion or grasp;

to grasp [the consequences of your inaction and seize the day] ;

to seize [the attention of the Universe by setting your intention to make change] ;

to make change in such a way as to impress favorably and deeply [yourself by the audacity of your action] ;

Sleeping in Truro

How are you a ghost here
when you were often only a conversation
words on a keypad
our ethernet tethers and ideals
someone I barely knew
save for a soft, full kiss on tiptoes   once
and the perfumed promise
of again and more
on a day that never came

but here, in Truro now,
your ghost whispers daily
of bourbon and dunes
the curve near Longnook
a family I never met

and Cassie at the Lobster Pot
you, even then, a shadow
of what might have been
those air wave words
"whatever she wants"
you told her,
a grand gesture
from two thousand miles away

i am a rock. i am an island.

One of a Thousand Lives

One sea gull drops its catch on the rocks
and I think there's a poem in that
but only the names have changed
since I last wrote a poem about the
one sea gull, its catch, and those rocks
that can be seen from the house
I thought for sure we'd buy
when it was for sale,
the year I wrote that poem about
the sea gull, its catch, and rocks

There was room there for
his design studio
and my writing space
for my art supplies
and his art collection
for his big dreams   and mine
a shared heart space

and that life   *oh that life*
was as beautiful then as this morning
the sea gull, its catch, those rocks,
and I, in starshine, nostalgic

74

Ephemera

The Wrong Impression

He ran, he told me,
through the corridors of Heathrow
the framed Monet under a free arm —
The Water Lily Pond
(to be precise) —
its soft curved bridge
symbolic, perhaps,
of his efforts to cross over
from friends
to something more colorful,
shall we say?
For the untrained eye
it gave the impression of love,
but look closely to see
a thousand random dots,
their missed connections
a terminal romance.

Illusion

I asked —
"Do you believe in magic?"
and he eagerly answered "yes,"
thinking his black and white dreams
were polychromatic like mine.

so I closed my eyes to pretend
his sleight of hand was enchanted
for as long as I could, but
there is no substitute for
lightning across a January sky.

Like Neurosurgery This Charge

Writing —
or trying to —
I found myself
remembering our secret.
You know,
the one that hides
beneath
your gray-templed,
sea-weathered hair.
That question mark scar
where the surgeon
opened a hole to your brain
with its sudden well of
life's elixir spilling forth.

Neatly sewn up now,
I wonder curiously
about the leak repaired
by expert hands.
Without like entry
I have no easy access
to time and memory.
No door on which to knock,
or portal for words —
only patience.
Resigned to wringing drops
of thought onto paper.

ephemera

Chester, 1:00 a.m.

You will always be blue flannel,

a plaid hard crush against skin,

Bourée on a flute in the dark,

and the taste of unseen spirits.

Your sudden kiss,

the punch-drunk dance

against kitchen counter —

what did you want from me

in that brief romance?

I still wonder.

Alternate Ending

As soon as I heard the tone of your voice

I knew I would change the story.

Right there, sitting on the step,

with the phone still warm against my ear,

I said out loud "It will not end this way."

I never looked back.

I just cut a hole through the wall,

and changed the language of doors.

Dear Jenny
For Joel (a.k.a. Hollywood)

Dear Jenny,

D'ya remember when you were fearless?
Ah sure do.
You fell in love with me as soon as my smile said
     hello to the fire in your eyes
and there weren't no stoppin' the combustion that was
     you, me, an' the open road ahead of us.
We were livin' an' lovin' those white line nights —
ain't no rules gonna stop a story like that drivin' itself,
from its firecracker first scene to its red hot goodbye.
An' all that wild fun we had in between?
You made me laugh like Ah ain't never laughed before.
Ah loved that sweet adventure, darlin'—
Ah'd do it again.
And you should too!
Don't go lettin' these ghosts scare ya.
You are Love an' Light an' Life.
Hell, you gave us *Life* — then
and here now on these pages.
You gave us Love, darlin', Love.
Don't you forget that never.

Come back,
"Hollywood"

The Consequence
of Rabbit Holes

84

Alice Falling

I am down the rabbit hole.
I am, I can feel it.
We are familiar with each other —
this weightlessness and I.

Tethers of knowing better
wave in the breeze
like red flags above my head

as
    I
        fall.

I will pretend
as long as I can
that I know the way back —
but I don't.

I never do.

I end up some place else.
Wonderland. Neverland.

Still, what I see in the looking glass
is as curious as she thought,
and it whispers *Adventures!*

as
    I
        fall.

Take the Pill if They Offer It, Alice

My doctor said she could give me a pill.
You know, before they cut me open to alphabetize my
    insides again?
That way I wouldn't know what hit me.

Hit, hurt, wound ⇨ isn't it all the same?
Here, there, inside, outside
everywhere all along after all?

They cut you open.
Leave you. Lie to you.
Break your heart.

End of the day, you're left with little pieces of you on the
    floor
and someone's gotta clean up the mess, remind you how to
    walk again.

Who wants to remember all of that?

Better to take the pill, swallow it down with an ocean of
    tears,
wake up smaller than you used to be, but not by all that
    much,
find some new adventure, have a party, drink
    some tea.

Housekeeping Anticipations

As if it matters
that her books are neatly arranged on the shelf,
the curtains washed and pressed, rehung.

Who will notice
the tea stain gone missing?
the cobwebs banished?

Is it for naught that she
fluffs the pillow where he will sit,
lays down summer sheets?

They are never as she expects
in the quiet rooms of her mind:
curious, engaged, layered with frosting.

But better to be hopeful —
set out cake plates just in case —
than throw it all out with the trash.

Putting Love Away

It's time to put love away.
I am twice shy to some
exponential degree,
bitten more than
I care to recall.
And there seems to be
no half-life
for the memories
that compound
as fertile compost
for the seeds
of these poems
you enjoy.
I am full to the brim
and ready for some
other folly now —

Tip me over and
pour me out!

Narrative Arc
ghost seven

A Knowing Way

He is water born,
bred with the taste of
salt on his tongue,
and sea air in his lungs.
He knows the
change of season,
the approaching storm,
the moment the water
will shimmer like glass.
The tide glides
through his veins,
in and out of a heart
that loves the water.
Loves the shoreline
that embraces
this deep, ancient brew.
Here, landbound,
he calls the trees by name,
speaks to birds of prey
both kin and ken,
in great companionship:
the sky his breath,
the woods and marsh
his hallowed refuge.

There Lies Truth

We lie in the dark
and whisper our truths,
when he asks:
What do you see
when you close your eyes?

I tell him I see
what I have always seen,
a vast expanse of stars,
like static at midnight
— *remember?* —
only dark and beautiful.

In the morning,
reports from Andromeda
show 100 million truths,
seeds of existence.

I see God, I tell him.
I see God.

narrative arc

Reading McKuen at Dawn

I am reading love poems this morning,
the smell of sleep still in my hair,
our last kiss lingering on lips
as I sip coffee and slowly turn pages
of someone else's memory.

There on yellowed white paper,
the poet catches moments not unlike
the ones you and I shared at 2
as we curled into each other,
blurring lines of you and me   and time.

I remember reading these poems
when love was paramount,
this poet's words my ideal,
set on a shelf with adolescent understanding
of supposed-to-be and meant-to-be.

How funny to turn these pages again,
beyond any year I could imagine then,
find companion with the poet
and the promise,
so certain I will turn a page
and find you there
reading lines,
my expressions of surprise.

Come Messy to This Parade

We do not apologize

for being unpracticed, unprepared, unzipped.

We often arrive out of tune, out of focus,
    out of our minds.

And still we settle into familiar step —

a stride, a pace, a cadence

of like heartbeats marking time.

Measuring Water by Sound

I want to know the color of your eyes, not just the browns
and greens of them, but by the specific Pantone colors of
their constellations.

I want to know by rote how your tongue forms the
syllables of my name, the way your lips make words in the
dark.

I want to know your skin like I know my favorite sweater,
how it caresses my shoulders, hugs my hips...where it rests
against my belly.

I want to know you by sound, the way I know I've
poured enough water in the pot for coffee we'll drink by
moonlight at three.

The Slow Migration of Love

My mentor tells me there is no escape from loving you. It's in my genes.

And while she goes on about brains and chemistry and the natural proclivity of species to procreate, I wonder...

Do birds redefine the space between wings to accommodate a change in flight so late in the season?

Do bees make sacrifices in the general order of things to find the sweetness of honey even as the days shorten?

Does the Monarch wax nostalgic for past lives, when she was everything — and nothing — but this?

Accommodations

how do we change?
accommodate?
make room?
or rooms?
is there even room?

is our space infinite
or finite?

can we build additions
into which we pour new foundations?

or rest on settlements
of stone and suffering?

beings of air and light
are never fixed, Love

even the ground spins
beneath our feet

Night Song
Lavender's blue, dilly dilly, Lavender's green...

Should the day ever come
when this story fades from the page,
let me discover your margin notes,
your penciled reminders
of nights scented with lavender,
when you sang *dilly dilly*
in the voice saved for those you love most.
That will be my keepsake,
pressed forevermore against the fold.

Under My Skin

I never feel bones resist
when we share skin.
Oh how easily
we slip into each other,
share the same space   and time

transcendent

remembering
your rib cage
that holy parting
as if it were yesterday
and today
and tomorrow

But in the quiet bed

alone

the endless space   and time
breaks bones
that pierce lungs
that make breath
to fill the silence.

Uncommon Dance

When you move to the beat of a different drum
there's no cure for the blister that forms
from the

dance
dance
dance

There's no common book on which to lean your fears
no vow that forgives the misdemeanors
of heart and soul
The way a fool would do...
Instead, you make a poultice from prayers
to no god and all gods,
a tincture of stardust and make-believe
to cool the heat of betrayal,
ease the disappointments,
and reconcile the little murders
you know he didn't mean.
Forget the relievers and remedies
for everything that ails you,
hide the scars with hope
pray this time   maybe
you'll both get it right.

narrative arc

Real Plums, Imaginary Cake

This morning
I baked a cake
from our dust and ashes
to see how it would taste.

Would it be harsh
or honeyed?

Would it coat
my lips with memory?

Licked and swallowed,
would it
fill up my belly
to curb this hunger?

Or would it catch
in my throat
smother words and breath

    this heartache

in sweet, sweet silence?

Memory Made

It is the building
that makes me whole —
my upright infrastructure.
They tell me it is bone,
sing songs that this
connects to that,
but how do you explain

the mystery pain
that takes up residence
in random places?

the cache they cannot see
with their machines
or diagnose with certainty?

the telltale whispers
in my head that haunt
and never relent?

narrative arc

the words that break off
from aftershocks
and fall at my feet,
collected in bowls
around my house?

I pick them up and write:
this is the labyrinth;
the year of sadness;
the walk on hallowed ground;
the day we saw whales
and he loved me because
I jumped for joy.

Long Weekend

It was New Hampshire
for God's sake
and I hoped it would imprint us
how could it not?
Those ridiculous mountains
their shock of snow
and sharp air so fresh
your lungs get greedy
But you were miles away
ghosts on your lead line
climbing summits of regret
backpack full of memories
bitter and sweet
stuck to the roof of your mouth
Which explains the dead silence
yours and mine
as we watched the snow fall
covering our footprints
on the path outside.

The Responsibility of Balloons

If one, for example,
is blessed with the gift,
of the most perfect balloon,
red or yellow or green
floating just so, just there
against the blue blue sky,
one must make all accommodations
to hold fast   steady fast
else that perfect thing
might slip from a grasp
with an *oh!* and a *no!*
and a sad, solemn watch
as it drifts   ever   so   far
out of reach.

Adjourned

Damn those little murders,
those small infractions
to which we pay no mind
save for the evidence marker
placed at the foot of the moment:
this, here, remember.

Wise or not wise we file them away
in a box called Misdemeanors
until the shelf bends and breaks
and proof bears witness;
only then do we see the trail
from that first red flag
to a catalog of minor injuries
and shallow stab wounds,
enough to leave us hobbled,
walking wounded.

In court, they'd present the facts
prove we didn't plan for this
to any known degree;
a crime of accident and
unintended consequences;
suggest ⇨ Self-Defense,
and we'd both without a word agree.

narrative arc

Apple of Discord

I had, for years,
chosen words carefully,
like one might apples
in the January bin —
hold, look, turn,
feel for the bruises
beforehand.
And I set them out
carefully
on the paper
we call a screen
so there was time
to savor my meaning —
hold, look, turn,
let down your guard,

love

But meaning proved
as elusive as the pests
that burrow in —
making scar tissue
unseen beneath the skin,
where bruises bloom
and hearts stay broke.

Narrative Arc

We blurred the shape of time,
bent it forward and back,
twisted it enough to find common ground
there in those early fairy tale days
when I was so astonished by Us I wept

Our movements so in sync
we seemed kindred,
some past-life edifice
full of favorite books and songs,
familiar stories — his and mine —
the ones we tell ourselves about Love
and who we are *in* Love

But I never thought to look up
see the turrets and towers along the wall,
pay note to the bunker safely guarded,
the pock marks in that common ground,
the mortally wounded specters
who watched their watches
betting on our time
our precious, precious time

I thought the enemy was age
that Loss would come as natural cause
     and effect, expected
a well-roundedness to its execution
but I was wrong

Loss seeped furtive between cracks I didn't
     know at first were there
forced itself into the weakest places of Us
the way ivy overtakes mortar in a wall
until all that was left was the evidence of time
     we call Memory.

They Called it a Microburst, But I Know Better

Across town, the sky was falling.
While I settled in
for the long, windy night,
he laid beneath fallen trees —
old trauma now compounded.

Everywhere, things were breaking —
foundations and forests —
and I wonder sometimes
if that was the moment
we broke as well.

The moment
all the cracks and shakes
finally   *finally*
split us apart.

These days,
in the forest where we
first and often met,
I can see our ruins —
mark the day of our beginning,
the warped rings of memory.
and in the wreckage of canopy,
our final silent fall.

narrative arc

**Sometimes Hearts Need Time
to Catch Up: A 100-Word Story**

I think, maybe, it's our ghosts I keep meeting in my
dreams. Not as often now as before, but still. They're
curled under a winter's weight of blankets, not daring
to move; reading by the fire with coffee before the sun
rises; walking through the woods on familiar paths, old
stories kicked around like leaves; sitting on lawn chairs in
the back yard before the big storm changed everything.
It's always he who reaches out for her hand, calls for her
attention. And she who closes her eyes and breathes it all
in — just one more time before I wake.

/ / /

Dreamwork

Dream Memory

Do you know me —
there before dawn,
as I wrap myself
around you and
savor your
one last dream?

You said memory
smells of cedar,
so I sleep
most nights
among the trees.

dreamwork

Évora Sunrise

#06-051113

Her silken robe
softly falls
from shoulders
on a balcony
by ruddy rows
of new-plowed crops.
Raindrops
dance down
window panes,
as Sparrow
sips nectar
from the hollow
of her collarbone.
Her voice only birdsong
when he calls for her
from the other side
of dreams.

January Dreamspace

#04-011114

the spirit in me
meets the spirit in you
there kitty-cornered
in the thought space
where Eames chairs
flank the walls
and a black and white
television hums
Synchronicity

dream room
waiting room
waystation

my baggage
is tucked neatly
in the overhead bin
so you can't see it
yours is, too,
but it's heavier
somehow — and dark

dream room
waiting room
waystation

it hurts to see you,
so I turn away,
but you hold me anyway
and we lie there
watching strangers pass —
this spirit in me
with the spirit in you

dream room
waiting room
waystation

When I am Dreaming, Come Kiss Me

#01-060514

The grass was damp, darling,
or I would have been there sooner.
I slipped back inside for slippers,
the silver ones you like so much.
Then up the ladder of branches I went,
to the path set down by stars,
straight North then left at Ursa Major.
I couldn't bear the thought of missing you,
so I skipped the clouds like hopscotch,
tossing raindrops at my feet —

jump so high, touch the sky
turn around, touch the ground

And there I was,
led by moonlight to your side.
"Tonight when I am dreaming, come kiss me,"
you were talking in your sleep.

"I just did," I whispered
as I woke to the day.

And They, in Repose

Pointing to the sky
overcast by fog,
he asks if I see Orion,
but I trip before I can look

and fall for him

So he lies down next to me
face so close
my breath steals his smile
and hides it beneath a rib
for safe keeping

And if I said you were beautiful...
he whispers to the shadows
that dance on the pavement
between our lips

The stars would fall, too

#01-061514

Not Much between Despair and Ecstasy

These pandemic dreams
are epicurean,
dipped in the deep steep
of slow surrender,
the lush brew of
spice and dirt,
bowls chin high
steam rising,
she and I on our small bed
in Shanghai
pressed tightly
together
in the fearless dark

or he, his
whiskered cheek
against my thigh,
tangled sheets
on his knees,
determined, despite
the warning siren,
the impending
firestorm,
the heat
of the sun
too soon
interrupting
the delicious
reverie.

dreamwork

Trickster Dreams, 2020
for MaryAnne

The fox who darted just out of eyesight yesterday
morning while I poured coffee is screaming

midnight screaming

so I half-wake, check for the cat, glance at the clock,
tumble back into our trip to New York

a brilliant spring day, sunshine and pink trees, a street
cafe/coffee shop amalgamation of people

it's pungent loud, crazy, and beautiful

You're up ahead buying a hand-knit mask, balancing your
coffee and flowered purse

I'm pacing by the India-print tunics on the phone with the
ex-lover only you know about, flirting in that way we do so
no one overhears

and before I can say I-Love-You-Goodbye again to you
there in the City on that wonderful city day or to him
again on the phone

I'm riding in a pick-up careening through the copse where
the screaming fox lives, smashing head-on into a great old
beech, its copper leaves jingling like bells to wake me for
the day.

I'd Really Like to Meet Her
for MaryAnne

There was snow
and she was her usual
ornery self about the matter —
I don't like snow
in a sweet huffy fit
mirroring her petulant
I don't like trees
when she'd sneeze.
How I miss all of that,
but I digress...

There was snow
and she was her usual:
the smile-and-laugh
approach to hard hard life,
a big and bold disguise
a wink even, I think,
and then she left.

She left and then
the bedroom light
turned on by itself
as a beam of sun
she never saw coming
poured through the window
and the radio lit for morning...

Tell me all your thoughts on God
'Cause I'm on my way to see her

dreamwork

Dream Collaboration

#05-072523

She knows, of course,
it's why she's allowed me here
this intimate task of parting,
of packing up your things,
why we smile easily
between hidden glances   *so this is her*

We've known each other forever,
wondered enough to troll,
but we're like minds and hearts
as well, why else
would you have loved us both?
I don't tell her I saw you
a shadow, a whisper
in her room,
that your smile
was in gratitude
for the kindnesses
here now, and then,
when I held tight your
sorrows and secrets.

Instead, we just laugh
at your photographs,
agree to keep the tape
in the top drawer
to put things back together
after I leave.

Late Night Visitor

#05-080323

He's been talking
in my sleep
every night this week,
pulls up a chair
next to the bed
and tells me
all of his thoughts
as if I am a vessel
for safe keeping
still, now
after all these years.

He wants to know
about the letters
he never wrote,
where I keep them and
asks questions
that make me laugh
out loud
from the dream.

dreamwork

I startle the cat
sleeping
in the crook
of my knees
who knows nothing
of our midnight ghost,
who wasn't here
when the story began
doesn't realize
there are no
pressed flowers
or souvenirs,
just words.

Just words
he'll never read,
pressed between
the pages of this book
        you hold in your hands.

Trapped
for DeLinda

#012524

I was trapped in a house of the past
where staircases appeared
twisting to nowhere
and rooms were puzzle games,

where I walked through
old conversations
and emerged in the present,
my foreign reflection
in a hall of faceless mirrors,

the scenes of people
I used to know
still in their old spaces
were so real I could touch
the pencil he held in his hand
at the desk he used to write from

dreamwork

but only she
only she
was my constant

broadcasting into rooms
to show me the way
with an urgent regard
so as not to get trapped there

hurried me to dress
and gather my things
as if the house were on fire

as if my insistence to stay
would alter a future
I still have no heart to imagine.

**At night, here in the library,
the ghosts have voices**

#07-112023

He's familiar somehow, though taller here in this
dreamspace, or maybe he's more than one — some
midnight rendering of them or Him —

but whatever he is, we're at the library — a colonnade
and chandeliers, passing spines and shelves

talking about books in a rambling conversation like
you have with that person who so easily takes up
the space next to you

remember?

I think I know him and love him — I must — because
when he leans in to kiss me I oblige

and we keep walking, out the door and through town
past nighttime store fronts for a while

until I wake up and wonder if I should perhaps
entertain the idea of a Him again

or if these midnight ghosts are company and substance
enough for the ten or twenty bit of road left ahead.

dreamwork

Muses

When the Mania Collapses in On Itself Again
for Janet

She — burning red on the outside rim
of a recent manic spin,
her hair in flames —
could not find space to fit
her guru self
anywhere in the cockpit,
left it and its
lowercase god
— the one she introduced me to —
somewhere in the space
where the inhale and exhale meet

But she was barely breathing
words shooting through the air
like   pew!   pew!   pew!
and her eyes...
her eyes were blazing madness

she was madness
at my doorstep burning
her counsel afire with delusion

I tried to reach out
breath like a blanket,
to swath the flames,
while my heart screamed
drop and roll! drop and roll!   *please*

please   come back

I reached into that space
her galaxy of lunacy,
but her trajectory
was light years from now

gone!

I hear she touched heaven
learned to breathe in a final breath
found peace as she dropped
into the hands of god

The Science of Women
for Lily Plisic, M.D., FACOG

There are small pink marks
softened with age
that only she will recognize,
knows how they adhere to time
and memory and this long, shared path.
She has seen me as no one else has—
vulnerable, prone, afraid —
allowed trust and autonomy
to dance even-step with
training and science.
Partners,
she ages with me now
gray for gray and line for line,
our nods of knowing
the flash, the sweat,
the weight of it all,
speak more than we ever have
in these brief encounters
these long precarious years
of waiting and watching
tell-tale scars fade.

**The Fleeting Moments of Light
(or When She is Allowed a
Visit to the Museum)**

Until she finds those
wide and wild brushstrokes,

Until her hands move
with air and light,

Until line and form
cease to define her,

We will stand in
the halls of masters,

Breathe

    her

        borrowed

            freedom

                like

                    air...

Star Prayer

In the east this night
great hero rises,
masked in bared trees
and mists of heaven.
The triad heralds
his arrival.

Today, we saw
stone titans
drawn out by glacier.
Triad, too, aligned
along our path,
in ancient wood,
by God's hands
or mechanism of man.

Stolen time for us,
this winter walk.
Spoken word and
friendship's pace
come easily now,
but time is precious
as life and blood bear down
on her with ties that bind
too tight to breathe.

The One in whose image
she was made
asked Job
"Can you loosen Orion's belt?"
on premise that He could.
Can she not, then?

Oh glorious
Alnitak! Alnilam! Mintaka!
Show her light
and give strength
that she may
find breath and
reach for the stars!

Love Thy Neighbor as Thyself

She worries most, she says
about salvation
— afterlife, eternal life —
rarely this one
this *wild, precious* one,
except about her
rights and wrongs,
her delicate walk
inside the lines;
says she worries
about me, too,
my wayward path,
its final stop,
but we agree
most days
to disagree,
find comfort in
our common path
of grade school steps
and wonderings,
of nature and of art,
of familiar faces
how we look the same
but probably don't
now 40 years gone by —
these are the things
that just won't change
come what may
and never mind.

Within the Confines

Maybe for breakfast you have *one* egg and toast *without*
    butter, and chai *without* whipped cream,
and maybe you swallow down the bitter truth of it with a
    token smile,
grab your bag from the hallway table, and escape into the
    crisp, cold morning air
breathe, breathe for a while
because you know at supper, after work, you'll only have
    one glass of wine, if that
and you'll take those things you brought home with you
    — the snips and pieces of passion — and tuck
    them back into that bag, that safe hiding place until
    tomorrow
so it's easier tonight to be one-note and unobjectionable,
hide your light, be small and of no consequence to
    anyone's conceit
so it's easier to say *no, no, no, it's OK* and *this is enough*,
    when what you should be saying is
I want orange marmalade and butter, please, sweet cream that
    whips to a peak, and three chilled glasses of Pinot, thank
    you very much.
I want to get up on that dance floor, darling, and make a
    complete fool of myself because one of us is leaving soon,
    and we won't get this chance again!

137

Breaking Bread 2020
for Mary

I miss the taken-for-granted pleasure of soft butter spread
on another piece of bread at my favorite restaurant, how
it complements the white wine served in a chilled glass so
well I could have a meal of just that: bread, butter, wine.

I miss the face of my friend across the table from me, less
than six feet for sure, her uncovered smile, the back and
forth of gestures, nods, hands-in-the-air exclamations
about all of those things:

art! writing! travel!
heron, hummingbird, bee!
life and love — and that bread, can you believe it?

I miss our slow, slow pace that lasts longer than a meal,
almost sometimes longer than a shift, as we nod our
gratitude to the waitress who knows us by smiles and
gestures that say

yes, pour more wine
yes, leave more butter, please
yes, yes more bread of course, more bread

when the only thing that covers our face is the brief glance
at a menu or the swipe of a linen napkin to wipe a crumb
from a smile never again taken for granted

We Are Two Kindred Spirits in August
for Judith

Can you just be, she says to me
and we do then, there
on a tepid summer Sunday,
throw out our lines
to catch hold the juggernaut
of passing time
slow it just enough
to eat curried pea soup
without spilling
and fresh raspberries
one   by   one,
from a crystal bowl,
to read poems
one   by   one   too,
until time comes to leave
and one   from   one   we part
for now and then and sometime yet again
soon, we hope, soon.

Wordsmiths over Coffee
for Dale

She says she is losing words
at her age, hard to come by

What is the name of that purple flower?

Crocus?

No. No.

She shrugs her shoulders as if to say:
I never wrote about flowers anyway.

Hyacinth?

I'm trying to put words in her mouth,
fill her up so she doesn't forget   or worse,
leave me behind to fill in the blanks myself.

Yes, Yes, that's it.

She nods and we laugh,
the pair of us relieved.

Hyacinth.

To Come Unbound
for Dale

Is envy
more or less sinful
than this
banal
attachment
to security?
For in her
I see
Sannyasa —
a holy
untethering
from
these
pedestrian
pursuits
heart   fully   here
and I am
full of awe.

Resilience Plan
for MaryAnne

It was supposed to be
the two of us —
forces of nature
against the winds,
sheltered in place
with the stories
only we remembered,
(or didn't anymore).
That was the contingency
if all else failed —
if our tethered moorings
proved futile against the currents.
We would make room
and accommodations,
adaptations we never mentioned,
save for who would get the couch
and who the chair where the cat slept,
who would pick the dance music,
and who would cook the roast chicken.
We hadn't prepared for
a sudden erosion of the familiar,
this unpredictable path
in a deep, cold surge of loss.

Walking Destiny's Fine Line
for MaryAnne

We didn't mention it that day,
the odd drag of the left foot
its sound like an after-thought...

second thoughts now
and too much time passed
to make a difference.

She never listened anyway
and who was I to
preach or teach or cajole?

We each bear our own weight
carry with us the things
we can't put down

and after a while they break us
prove too much for this fragile vessel
that bursts into a thousand stars.

Our destiny is all of that, right there,
following us around with an odd echo drag
few of us ever, ever mention.

Missing Banksy
for MaryAnne

I gave short notice to the
street art
graffiti
work of art
outside the subway station.

I figured we'd
see it
catch the R train
walk this way
again at some point.

Then we would have time for
admiration
reverence
gratitude

But Banksy is what I forget, the
change
impermanence
fleeting nature
of this river ever flowing.

The Final Ghost

Did You Love?
for my Dad, who gets the last word

When you were little,
you called
downtown's
smokestacks and steeples
The Amazing City
despite its despair.

Did you keep that open heart?

And when you were five,
you learned, no matter the fall,
the crash, the number of stitches
to sew up the pain,
you get right back to it.

Did you keep trying?

When you were eight,
you started on your path —
you know, the out of step,
different drum,
on your own two feet path.

Are you still dancing?

the final ghost

When you were young
you loved
your stories
the fairy tales and magic,
those long, winding
conversations
with your imagination.

Did you keep dreaming?
Did you keep believing?

Did you love?

And did you keep loving?

148

Endnotes

endnotes

Doerr, Anthony. *Memory Wall: Stories*. United Kingdom: Scribner, 2011.

Erickson, Victoria. *Edge of Wonder: Notes from the Wildness of Being*. Canada: Enrealment Press, 2015.

Kintsugi is the Japanese art of repairing broken pottery by mending the areas of breakage with lacquer dusted or mixed with powdered gold, silver, or platinum. As a philosophy, it treats breakage and repair as part of the history of an object, rather than something to disguise.

Time Traveler, 2013 and **There is No Synonym for Reunion** owe thanks to Gene Roddenberry and the Star Trek universe.

Rockport mentions the Garth Brooks song "The Dance" (1989), written by Tony Arata.

I prayed he left more than a spoon was written with a deep bow of gratitude to the serendipity of the movie *Same Time, Next Year*.

The inspiration for the poem **Heist** was a poster called *Viva Terlingua!* A promotional poster from the 2010 Original Terlingua Chili Championship, it showed a woman in a "bright red cowboy hat, hand-strung turquoise beads and that witty West Texas smile" painted by Frank X. Tolbert 2. In a bit of what-a-small-world, the person I emailed to inquire about the artist turned out to be not only the artist's sister but also the woman in the painting —Kathleen Ryan! And...when she read and shared the poem with her colleagues, I was invited to be a judge at the next Chili Championship. (Unfortunately, COVID got in the way of that adventure.)

Both **Heist** and **Dear Jenny** are best read with a southern-ish cowboy drawl.

Ode to My Ghost at Terlingua (or You Just Keep on Pushing My Love Over the Borderline) appears with thanks to Madonna, Moses, Matthew 5:30, and Third Eye Blind.

Under His Spell recounts true stories, those sharp moments we always remember, as if we've been enchanted.

Codepend-dance moves along with a nod to Aerosmith, Gene Kelly, and the movie *Dirty Dancing*.

Just Once in a Very Blue Moon includes excerpts from the song "Once in a Very Blue Moon," written by Eugene Albert Levine and Patrick Alger, as sung by heavenly Nanci Griffith on the *One Fair Summer Evening* album (1988).

15 Years Fast Forward reappears here from my book *Water Under the Bridge: A Sort of Love Story* modified poetically to fit.

What if LA LA LA Is My Superpower? includes a reference to the Green Day song "Give Me Novocain" from their amazing (and cathartic) *American Idiot* album.

endnotes

The title of **Just Forget the World** comes from the song *Chasing Cars* by Snow Patrol.

The Road to Damascus is used here as reference to an important moment of insight, one that leads to a dramatic transformation of attitude or belief, but there are biblical/ religious overtones (i.e. apostle Paul's conversion on the road to Damascus) that echo in this chapter.

The chapter title — **I Am a rock. I Am an island.** — is a nod to the Simon and Garfunkel song from the 1960s that talks about isolation and emotional detachment as a way to avoid pain and brokenheartedness.

Sleeping in Truro is about a haunting in Truro, Massachusetts on Cape Cod.

In the poem **Chester, 1:00 a.m.**, *Bourée* refers to Jethro Tull's 1969 flute-based adaptation of the song written by Johann Sebastian Bach.

Background music in **Putting Love Away** is "I'm a Little Teapot," and in **Uncommon Dance** it's "Heart & Soul."

A Knowing Way and **Star Prayer** both appeared in my book *Evidence of Flossing: What We Leave Behind*.

Reading McKuen at Dawn refers to the poet and song writer Rod McKuen, popular in the 1960s.

Measuring Water by Sound first appeared in the international anthology *Coffee Poems: Reflections on Life with Coffee* (World Enough Writers, 2019)

The Night Song is "Lavender's Blue," an English folk song and nursery rhyme from the 17th century, sung in the poet's mind by Burl Ives.

Real Plums, Imaginary Cake cuts its title from novelist Mary McCarthy's quote about the task of writing, "I am putting real plums into an imaginary cake."

The poems in **DREAMWORK** include notations for ghosts and dates of the actual dreams. (i.e. #06-021413 is Ghost Six, February 14, 2013)

Évora Sunrise appears in Évora, a town in Portugal to which I have never traveled except in a dream.

January Dreamspace is (ironically, thinks the poet) filled with music by The Police.

When I am dreaming plays with a familiar children's nursery rhyme.

Not much between despair and ecstasy owes its title to Murray Head's song "One Night in Bangkok."

I'd Really Like to Meet Her is a line from the Dishwalla song, "Counting Blue Cars," that plays when the radio wakes the poet.

endnotes

At night, here in the library, the ghosts have voices is a quote from the Alberto Manguel book *The Library at Night*.

In **Star Prayer**, Alnitak, Alnilam and Mintaka are the names of the three stars in the constellation Orion's belt.

Thank you Mary Oliver for the *wild, precious* lines in **Love Thy Neighbor as Thyself** borrowed from her poem "The Summer Day."

Resilience Plan and **Walking Destiny's Fine Line** first appeared in my book *Waiting Out the Storm*.

With gratitude to my muse, who gave me the final ghost, **Did You Love?**

I am a part of all that I have met, from Alfred Tennyson's "Ulysses":

> *I am a part of all that I have met;*
> *Yet all experience is an arch wherethrough*
> *Gleams that untraveled world whose margin fades*
> *Forever and forever when I move.*

Wallace, David Foster. *The Pale King*. United States: Little, Brown, 2011.

Index of Poems

160

with gratitude...

To my Mom, the storyteller.

To Nan Meneely for her time,
heart, and good counsel.

To Judith Bruder, Tara Buckley,
DeLinda Spain, and Mary O'Connor
for helping me shepherd the ghosts.

To Malgorzata Maj for the gift
of your breathtaking cover
photograph. I have loved it for years!

To Michael Rayback for lending images
to the words. I pray you are safe.

And to the ghosts and muses...
I am a part of all that
I have met, my loves.

Always.
♥

162

about the artists

Malgorzata Maj (Mrągowo, Poland)
www.sarachmet.com

Lana Elanor (Tulume, Mexico)
www.etsy.com/shop/LanaElanor

Michael Rayback (Kyiv, Ukraine)
www.creativemarket.com/michaelrayback

Dear Reader,

Thank you for reading *Sleeping with Ghosts*!

This has been a labor of love...quite literally. I think writing memoir demands that. It asks that you revisit your past, that you be present in those old stories in such a way that you fall in love again...with the persons, the relationships, the experiences.

More than anything, writing memoir requires you to be brave. To stand with arms outstretched, ready to welcome back the moments that made you who you are today with an open heart and a willing pen.

What you hold in your hands is my best recollection of the ghosts who frequent my dreams, fill my heart, and wander in my memory, always.

I hope you enjoyed meeting them!

More than anything else, I hope you find inspiration to bravely tell your own stories!

With Love,

♡ Jen

Jen Payne
randomactsofwriting.net

Check out my website,
randomactsofwriting.net, or
get in touch if you have questions,
wordsbyjen@gmail.com.

Be sure to sign up for my quarterly
newsletter *Creatively Speaking*
(tinyurl.com/4creativelyspeaking)

If you are so inclined, I would be very
grateful if you would write a review.
You can find me on Bookshop.org,
Amazon, Goodreads, and Barnes & Noble.

You can also follow me
on Facebook and Instagram.

Go to linktr.ee/jenpayne or click
on the QR code below to see a complete
list of my website and social media links.

every love story is a ghost story

DAVID FOSTER WALLACE

JEN PAYNE is inspired by those life moments that move us most — love and loss, joy and disappointment, milestones and turning points. When she is not exploring our connections with one another, she enjoys contemplating our relationships with nature, creativity, and spirituality. Ultimately, she believes it is the alchemy of those things that helps us find balance in this frenetic, spinning world.

In addition to *Sleeping with Ghosts*, Jen has published four books: *LOOK UP! Musings on the Nature of Mindfulness*, *Evidence of Flossing: What We Leave Behind*, *Waiting Out the Storm*, and *Water Under The Bridge: A Sort-of Love Story*.

Her work has been featured in numerous publications including the international anthology *Coffee Poems: Reflections on Life with Coffee*, the Guilford Poets Guild *20th Anniversary Anthology*, *Waking Up to the Earth: Connecticut Poets in a Time of Global Climate Crisis*, the *2024 Connecticut Literary Anthology*, and *The Perch*, a publication by the Yale Program for Recovery and Community Health.

Jen is the owner of Words by Jen, a graphic design and creative services company she started in 1993, based in Branford, Connecticut — where she keeps house with a cat named Molly. She is a member of the Arts Council of Greater New Haven, the Connecticut Poetry Society, the Guilford Art Center, and the New England Poetry Club.

Books from Three Chairs

Sleeping with Ghosts
Poems & Musings
Jennifer A. Payne

Say Yes! to Your Creative Self
Insights, Illustrations & Prompts
Mary O'Connor

From My Button Box: Collected
Essays in a Pandemic Time
Judith Bruder

Water Under the Bridge
A Sort-of Love Story
Creative Non-Fiction
Jennifer A. Payne

Waiting Out the Storm
Poetry Chapbook
Jennifer A. Payne

Evidence of Flossing:
What We Leave Behind
Poems & Photos
Jennifer A. Payne

Look Up! Musings on the
Nature of Mindfulness
Essays & Photos
Jennifer A. Payne

www.3chairspublishing.com

Three Chairs
PUBLISHING™

Creative Conversations in Print

NEW! from
Mary O'Connor

NEW! from
Jen Payne

NEW! from
Judith Bruder

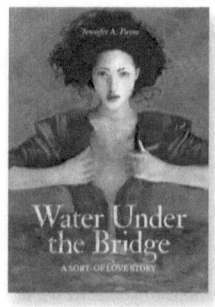

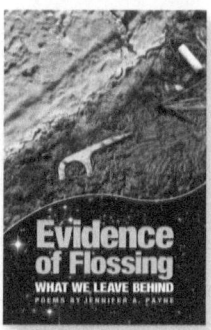

www.ingramcontent.com/pod-product-compliance
Lightning Source LLC
Chambersburg PA
CBHW030255130626
46549CB00002B/540